RAD TATS

GUNSHOW VOLUME 4

Published by TopatoCo Books
A division of The Topato Corporation

116 Pleasant St. Ste 203
Easthampton, MA 01027

gunshowcomic.com
topatoco.com

PRINTED IN CANADA, April 2013, First Printing

ISBN-13: 978-1-936561-05-6

10 9 8 7 6 5 4 3 2 1

craiglist search for skull and remember to delete your history

the skull has no mercy

Did you remember the bagels?!

who approved this loan to a rude dog?? Dogs don't know its not loans!!

OKAY, LOOK.

WHAT.

CHOMF

DO YOU *SEE* THAT! WHAT THE *FUCK* IS THAT?!

IT'S A... CAT TAKING A LUNCH BREAK.

I GUESS

'okay well, i'm gonna stay a bit longer.'

or you coulda just blogged about it.

slide-whistle

did you eat your black eye peas for the new year or are you a bad son.

HOURS LATER...

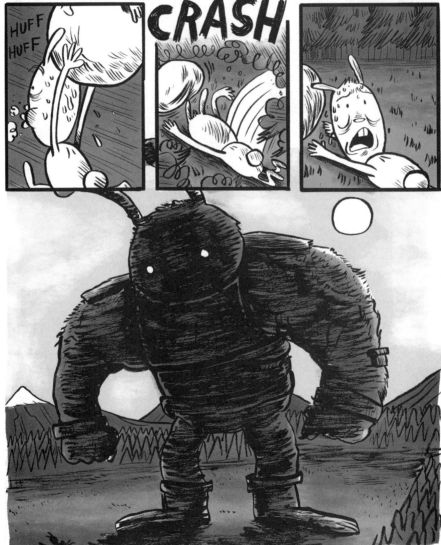

shadow of the rabbossuss or shadow of the colosubbit or whatever it doesn't matter

lets see some bananas and nuts

HE IS STUCK

GO, MY RABBIT FRIEND,

GO!

WOAH!

GO! FIND THE WEAK SPOT!!

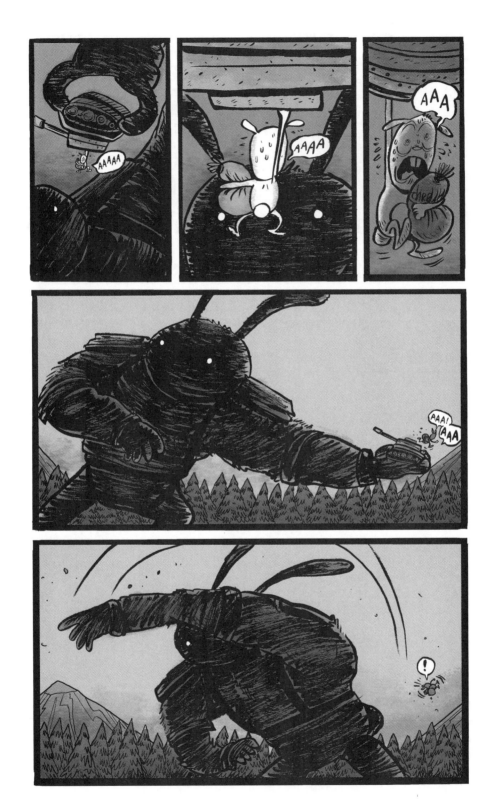

AW-HAAAWWW NO MORE TANK.

WELL, I CAN JUST SPAWN ANOTHER—

YOU HAVE BEEN KICKED FROM THE SERVER.

38

Invest those carrots for a brighter future, young rabbit

THIS IS IT, FELLAS.

THIS IS THE SPOT WHERE MY HOROSCOPE TOLD US TO STAND IF WE WANTED...

TO DIE.

CUT IT WITH THE THEATRICS, PAUL. WE HAVEN'T GOT THE TIME.

LET'S KILL OURSELVES ALREADY

THE SUICIDE CLUB

MICKEY

DICK

ROGER

PAUL

42

oh there's where that tank went.

44

we'll make boner soup.

SOME KIND OF... BOTCHED SUICIDE PACT WITH THE WIFE...

...OR SOME-THING.

MAN, WHO CARES!!

I CAN'T FOCUS ON THESE DEAD BODIES NOW THAT WE HAVE THESE--

RAD TATTOOS.

YEAH, I KNOW WHAT YOU MEAN.

TATTOOS?

YEAH! WE WERE GONNA GET BIG ONES ON OUR FACES...

YEAH, LIKE ALL...
"FUUUCK YOOOOOU,
LOOK AT IT."

...BUT WE OPTED FOR TRAMP STAMPS.

WANNA SEE?!

N-

-O.

the trashiest tattoo on the ugliest backfat

 ...HEY, THIS IS KIND OF LIKE A NEW YORKER CARTOON, HUH?

WHY DO YOU KEEP SAYING THAT?

I DON'T ALWAYS—

NO. YOU DO.

EVERY CASE WE'VE HAD THIS WEEK HAS ENDED WITH YOUR INSISTENCE THAT OUR LIVES ARE LIKE A NEW YORKER CARTOON WHICH IS VERY—

DOCTOR, COME QUICK! THE MAN IN THE OTHER ROOM IS HAVING A WHITE PERSON PROBLEM!

OH, GREAT. NOW I'M GONNA HAVE TO DELETE HIS TWITTER ACCOUNT.

SNAP.

BUT SERIOUSLY, CUT IT OUT

Later...

"Coffee cures my daily brain rot!"

'christ, what an asshole'

"NOW THEY WANT THE WAZOO!"

AND I JUST GOT THAT SEWED SHUT LAST MONTH!

SO PLEASE, IS THERE ANYTHING THAT CAN BE DONE ABOUT MY TAXES THIS YEAR?

SIR, WE HAVE THIS ALL TAKEN CARE OF! YOU NEED NOT WORRY.

OH GREAT CUS I WAS FREAKIN' OUT FOR A—

WE HAVE OUR BEST WRITER ON YOUR STORY.

WAIT, WHAT DID YOU SAY.

ONLY THE HOTTEST NEW WRITER HAS BEEN ASSIGNED TO YOUR TAXES, SIR.

HIS NAME'S DAVID BREAKFAST AND HE'S FRESH OUT OF GETTING KICKED OUT OF COLLEGE.

THE ONE ACT PLAY HE WROTE DURING THAT TIME WAS PHENOMENAL, BREATHTAKING...

...AND ALSO THE REASON HE CAN'T GET BACK INTO HIS SCHOOL.

SHUT.

YOU GAVE MY TAXES TO SOME KID?!

OF COURSE! HE'S USING THE INFO FROM YOUR TAX DOCUMENTS TO WRITE THE STORY OF YOUR LIFE!

AND RIGHT NOW, WE NEED YOU TO SIGN OFF ON A FEW PROPS NEEDED FOR—

WAIT, WAIT.

I CAME HERE TO GET *HELP* ON DOING MY TAXES AND FILING THEM! I THOUGHT YOU GUYS WERE *TAX PROS.*

LIKE THE SIGN SAYS OUTSIDE!

SSSSIIIGNNN...

YES, YOUR—

TAX PROSE

OKAY SO THE VISUAL IMAGERY OF THE DENOUEMENT WILL REQUIRE 16 CATS AND THE BAKER'S BIGGEST MUFFIN.

Prose before Hos, or if you're gay, go with Prose before the Hose. You're welcome.

"Of course we fax!"

ford the river !! You lost one (1) pizza.

anched-oavies and pipe aples

YES, I WANTED... WANTED TO LET YOU KNOW THAT THERE ARE... DISCREPANCIES IN THE COMPANY FUND.

TO PUT IT BLUNTLY, WE'RE HEMORRHAGING MONEY.

AND I HAVE REASON TO BELIEVE...

...TO BELIEVE THAT IT'S AN *INSIDE JOB!*

SOMEONE IS EMBEZZLING LARGE SUMS OF MONEY FROM THE COMPANY!

AND... UH.

TH-THAT'S IT.

FWOOO

WHO ELSE HAVE YOU TOLD ABOUT THIS?

yucky dog booms. the grossiest.

66

who's gonna pick up those flowers? what a mess.

WELL AT LEAST YOU HAVE THE PASSION, FOX, BUT I'LL ADMIT THIS...

...I HAVEN'T A *CLUE* ABOUT WHERE TO EVEN BEGIN ON TAKING THIS COMPANY DOWN.

KNOCK

THAT'S IT!

Did you even remember to bring the GUTS BAG?

someone in the back then shouted 'SOMETIMES WHY!'

THERE YOU ARE! I HAVE A PROBLEM!!

I *THINK* I SEXUALLY HARASSED A TINY ANIMAL THAT WORKS HERE...

COULD...

THEY...

...DOCK MY PAY FOR DOING THAT

YOU WON'T EVEN GET PAID ANYMORE WITH THIS COMPANY GOING THE WAY IT IS NOW!

TOSS

she's running over to check if anyone answered her post on
Yahoo Answers about sexually harassing a tiny animal.

76

HA HA! THIS IS PERFECT! IF WE CAN KEEP THIS UP, THE WHOLE BUSINESS WILL BURN DOWN IN *NO TIME!*

HA HA

HIM!

BAM!

I HAD A FEELING HE WAS BEHIND THIS!

WHO? WHO IS THAT?

UHHHH UH UH

HE'S A RIVAL... FROM MY OLD BUSINESS, YEAH! HE'S A STRAIGHT-UP *JERKO* AND HE *HAS* TO BE THE ONE!

THE ONE WHO DONE UP AND EMBEZZLED US.

TASTE THE PAIN

THAT'S WHAT EMBEZZLED MEANS?!

HOW DID YOU BUY A COMPANY AND **NOT** KNOW WHAT THAT MEANT?!

FAKE IT 'TIL YOU MAKE IT, I GUESS.

WHERE ARE YOU GOING?

I'M GOING TO CHECK ON MY INITIAL INVESTMENT! THE BAG OF CARROTS I TOOK FOR MYSELF TO BUY THIS COMPANY!

AND IF I FIND OUT SOMEONE'S BEEN SNEAKIN' AN EAT AT MY CARROTS, THEY'RE GONNA BE **HELLA DEAD.**

OH GOOD! WHEW!

LOOKS LIKE EVERYTHING IS OKAY, AFTER ALL!

WHAT ARE YOU TALKING ABOUT?! EVERYTHING'S GONE!!

YEAH, I'VE BEEN SAVORING THOSE CARROTS SINCE I BOUGHT THE COMPANY! LITTLE BY LITTLE, EATING AWAY AT THEM AND ENJOYING THE VICTORY!

TOO BAD THIS IS THE LAST OF 'EM, BUT AT LEAST THE SCARE OF AN EMBEZZLER TURNED OUT TO BE FALSE!

NO IT ISN'T!!

YOU'RE THE REASON THE COMPANY'S LOSING MONEY!! YOU'VE BEEN EATING IT!!

YOU'RE THE EMBEZZLER!

WHAAAA

that last panel is you, right now.

on the next, arrest rabbit development *fox drives the stair-car into the jail*

knock knock are you wompin in there?! *knock* quit that wompin in there, you'll womp your eye out!!

88

Old Man Pointing Up and Also Pointing Down (fig. 1)

90

They find her a week later, amid a pile of empty fire extinguishers, bored out of her mind.

Fox just broke rule number 1

OKAY LLLADIES, IT'S JAIL BREAK TIME!

WE'RE GONNA DIGG THIS SOFT PATCH OF DIRT LIKE IT WAS A CUTE VIDEO OF A BABY DUCK.

TAKE YOUR SHOVELS AND--

GO!

IF WE KEEP DIGGIN' IN THIS DIRECTION,

WE'LL HIT ONE OF THE GUARD TRUCKS AND WE CAN ESCAPE!

A CHINESE RESTAURANT? WE OVERSHOT IT!

TOO MANY WITNESSES! KEEP DIGGIN'!

What TIME is it! Who stole my watch! Fuck!

AH CHEER UP, FRIEND. LOOK AT IT THIS WAY:

IN THE LONG RUN, THE BIG THINGS THAT HAPPEN IN YOUR LIFE DON'T MEAN SQUAT.

IN THE END, YOU'LL STILL BE HAPPY WITH THE CHOICES YA MADE T'GET WHERE YOU ARE.

THIS WILL BE THE BEST THING THAT HAS EVER HAPPENED TO YOU. YOU WILL ALWAYS FIND A WAY TO BE HAPPY.

OR HOW ABOUT I TELLS YOU A STORY OF A SCHMUCK WHOSE GOT IT WORSE THAN THE BOTH OF US?

CLAP CLAP

HEH! ALL RIGHT, THEN! T'REALLY GET AN IDEA OF THIS GUY'S LIFE, WE NEED T'GO BACK TO THE BEGINNING.

HIS BIRTH.

'okay now put it back'

HOW DO YOU THINK I FEEL TAKING HIM OUT *IN PUBLIC*. THE LOOKS I GET, JERRY. THE *LOOKS*.

I KNOW, BUT

WE CAN'T JUST GIVE UP ON HIM, HE'S STILL A BABY.

UUUUGGH

AND ALL THE ORPHANAGES I CALLED HAVE A STRICT RULE ABOUT THIS.

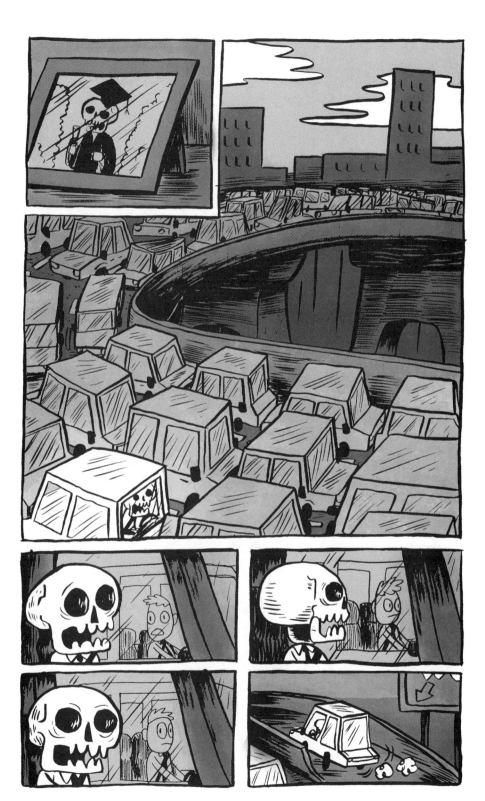

'Duck, take me to the fax machine. We have a pizza to order.'

JAB!

Two Skulls Kissing, Big Tongue dot mpg

extra comics

i ate so much that my gut has become it's own religion.

YES, SIR. JUST EGGNOG.

YOU SEE... I GUZZLED TWO GALLONS OF IT IN THE BATHROOM DURING THE RECESS.

EGGNOG OR GO TO HELL

KC GREEN

draws a bit here and there.
sometimes. whenever. who
knows.

illustration of the author by
Matt Cummings • eiffelart.ca

TOPATOCO™

PROUD PURVEYOR OF WEBBED COMICS ALL OVER THE UNIVERSE

DINOSAUR COMICS
by Ryan North
Dinosaur Comics is a comic about dinosaurs and friendly good times! It stars T-Rex, who likes to stomp on things such as houses and cars and humans, and Utahraptor, who likes to tell T-Rex that this is not such a good idea. It uses the same pictures in every comic with just the words changed! It is Better Than It Sounds.
books: topatoco.com/qwantz
read online: qwantz.com

AMAZINGSUPERPOWERS
by Wes Citti & Tony Wilson
What do radioactive goats piloting bomber jets, infants irreedeemably infatuated with 1970s game-show hosts, and sentient valve cover gaskets have in common? None of them are in this book! At least, I don't think so. Dare you find out for yourself?
books: **topatoco.com/asp**
read online: **amazingsuperpowers.com**

NEDROID PICTURE DIARY
by Anthony Clark
Beartato is a bear who is also a potato. His best friend is a bird-man. Sometimes there is a walking shark or a mean dog. Don't worry! This is almost entirely made-up.
books: topatoco.com/nedroid
read online: nedroid.com